PARIS
COLORING BOOK

30 HAND DRAWN, DOODLE AND FOLK ART STYLE SECRET PARIS THEMED ADULT COLORING PAGES

ISBN-13: 978-1537082042
ISBN-10: 1537082043

Aimer Manger
Paris

Au

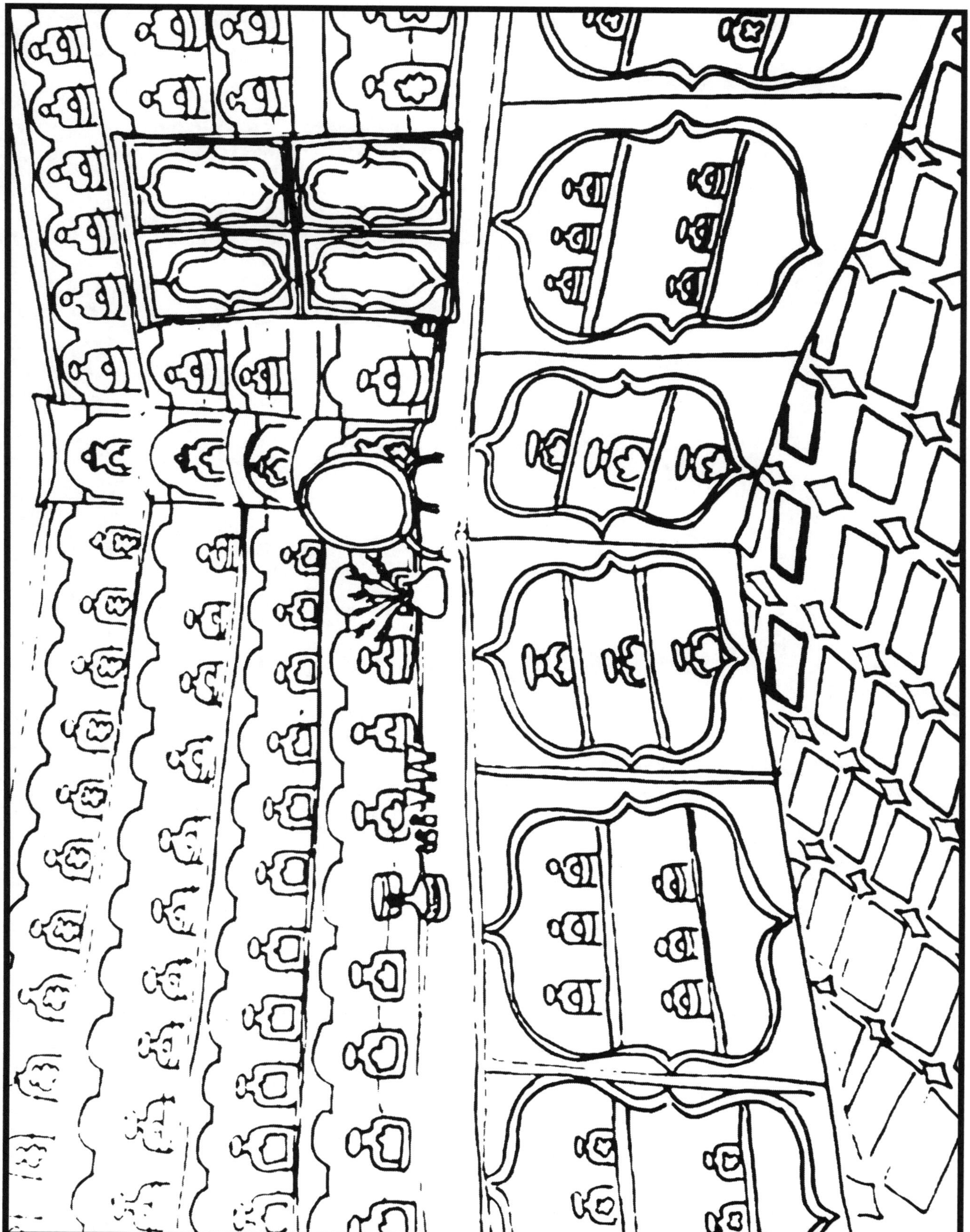

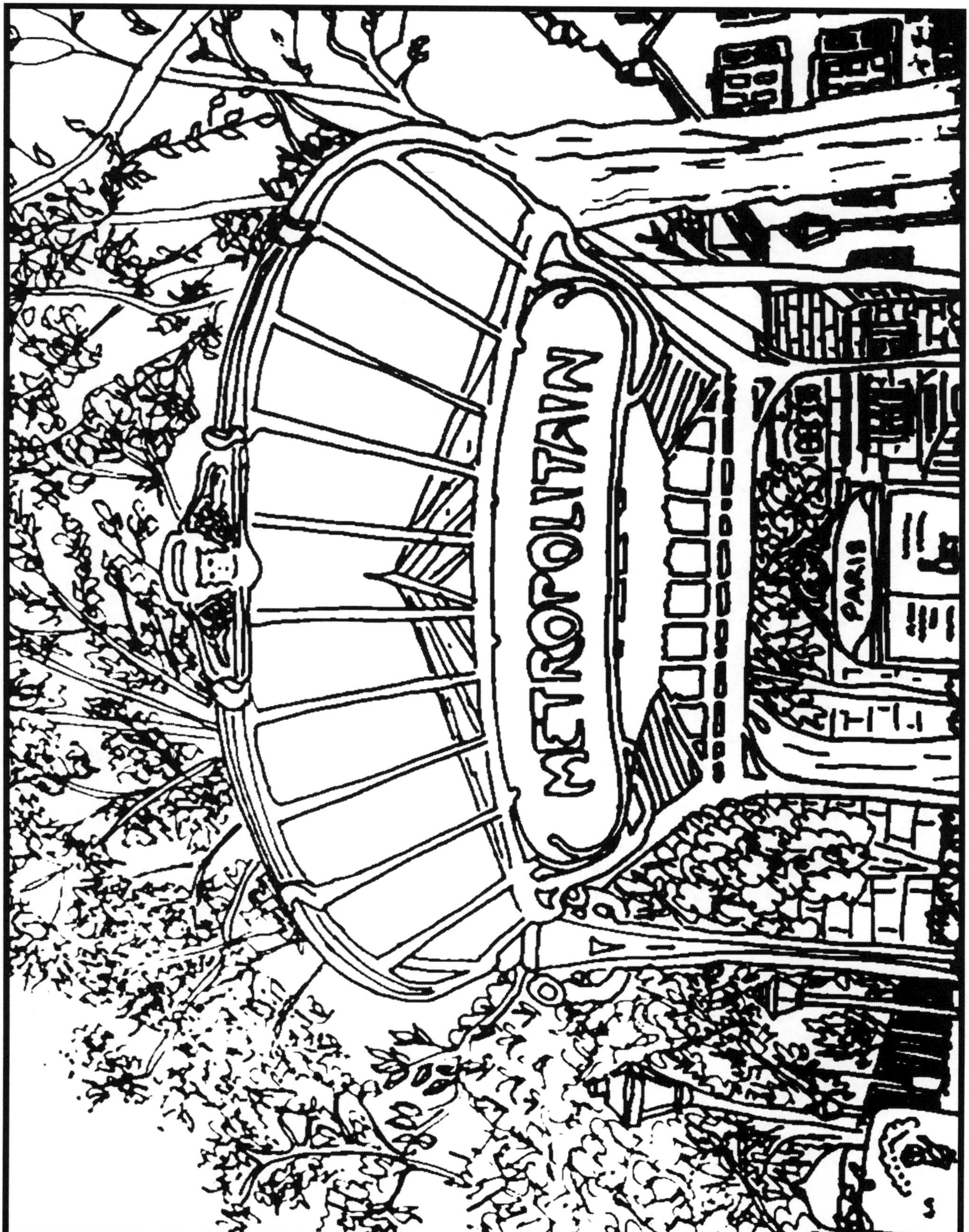
METROPOLITAIN
PARIS

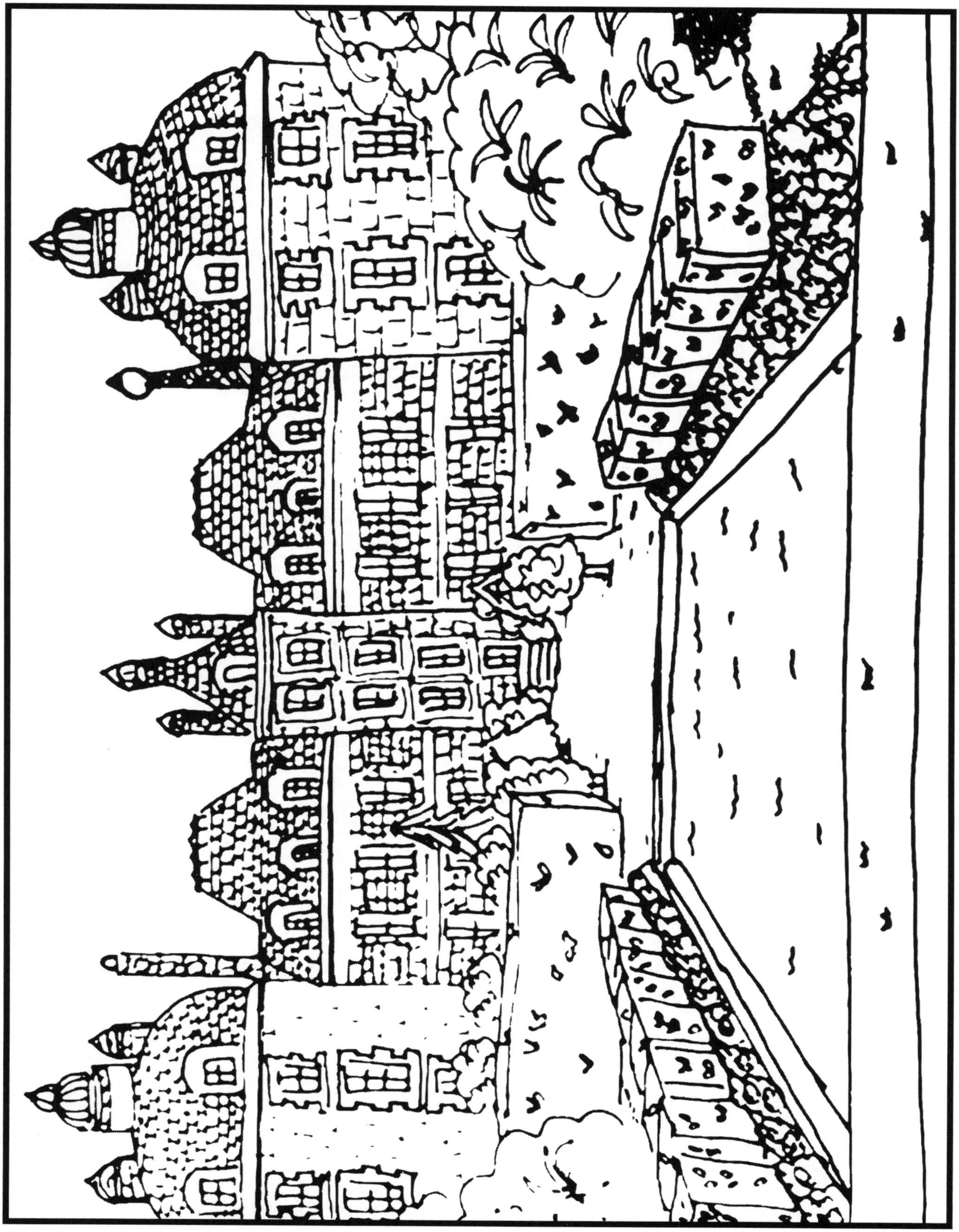

Lapérouse
RESTAURANT
Lapérouse

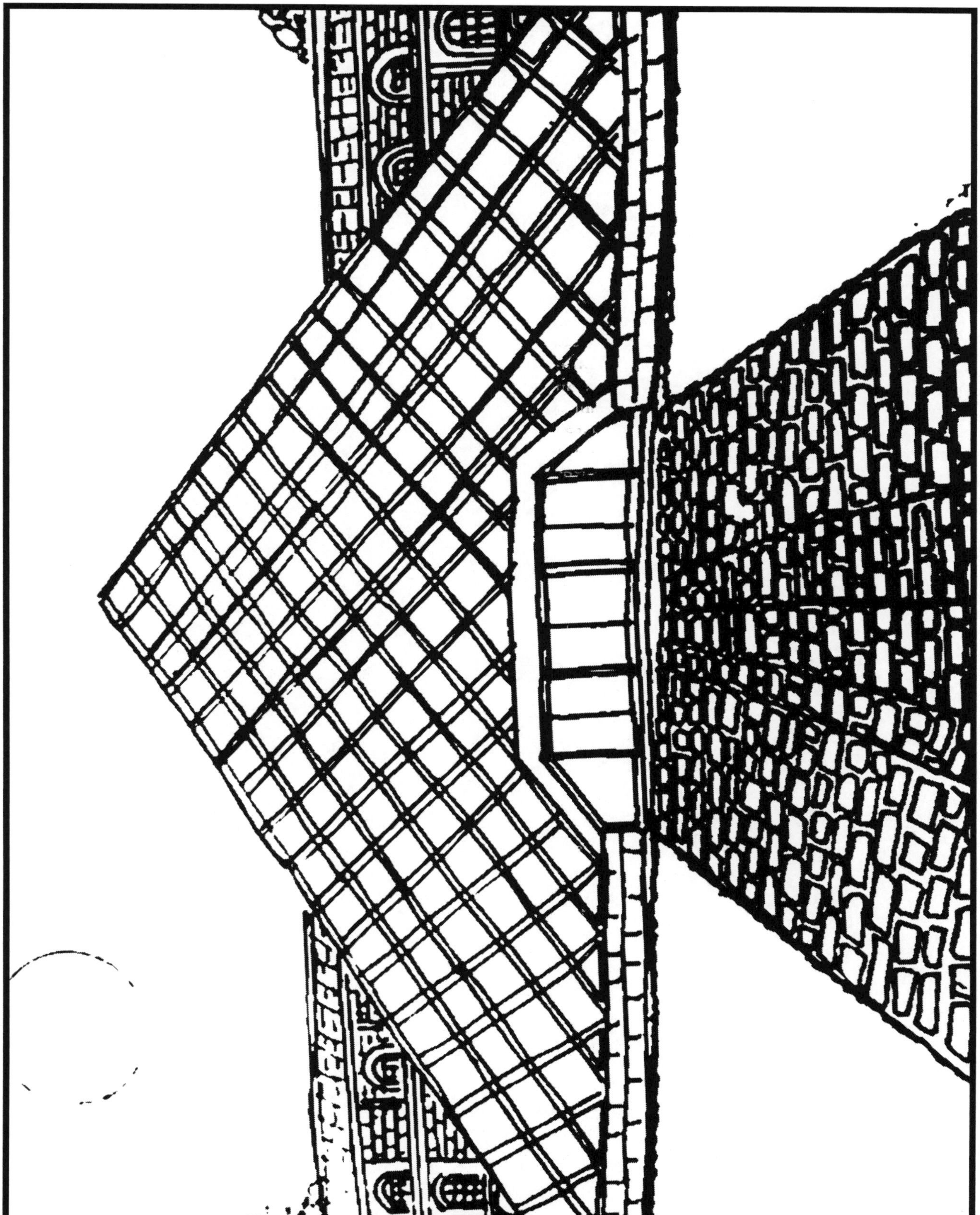

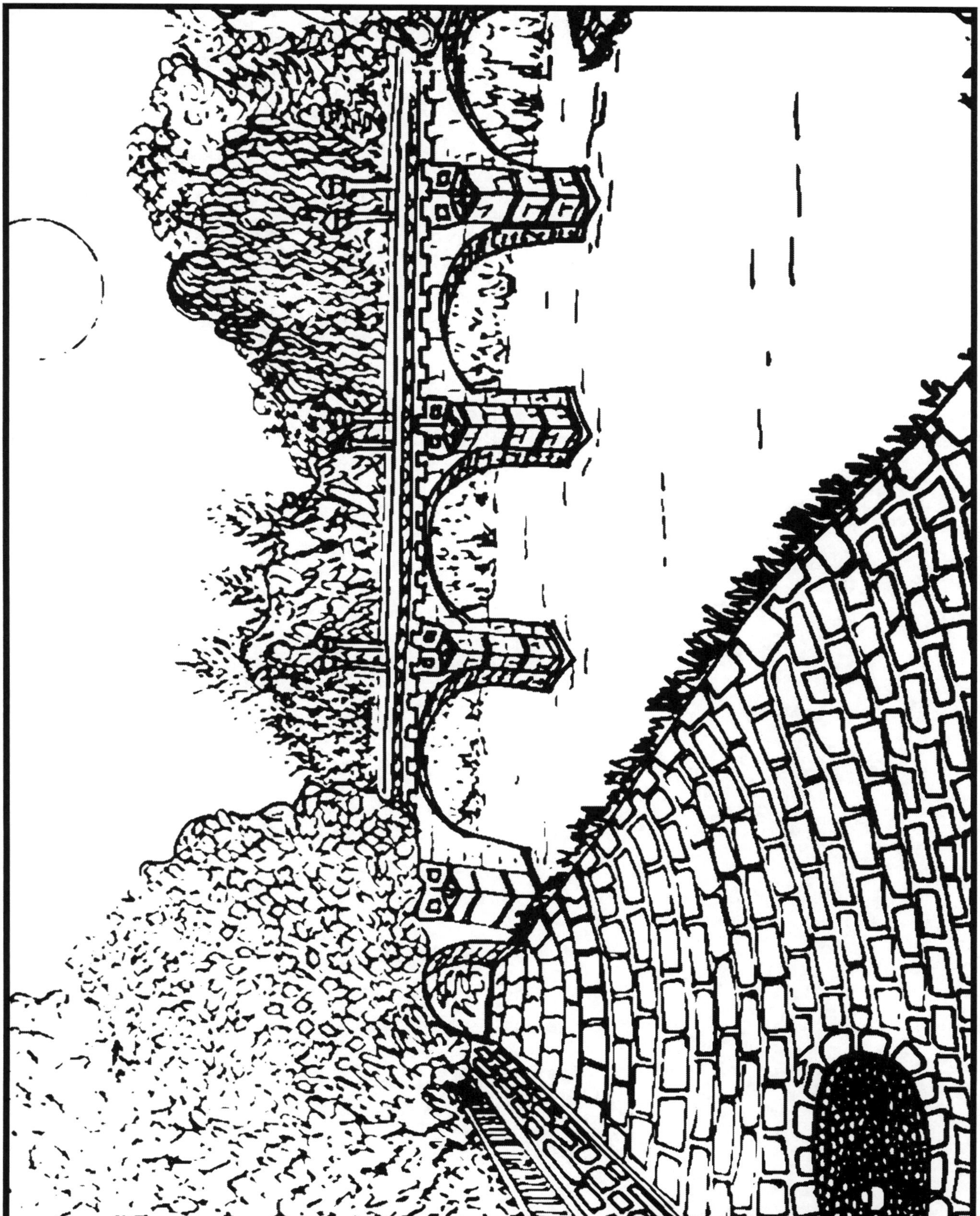

fleuriste

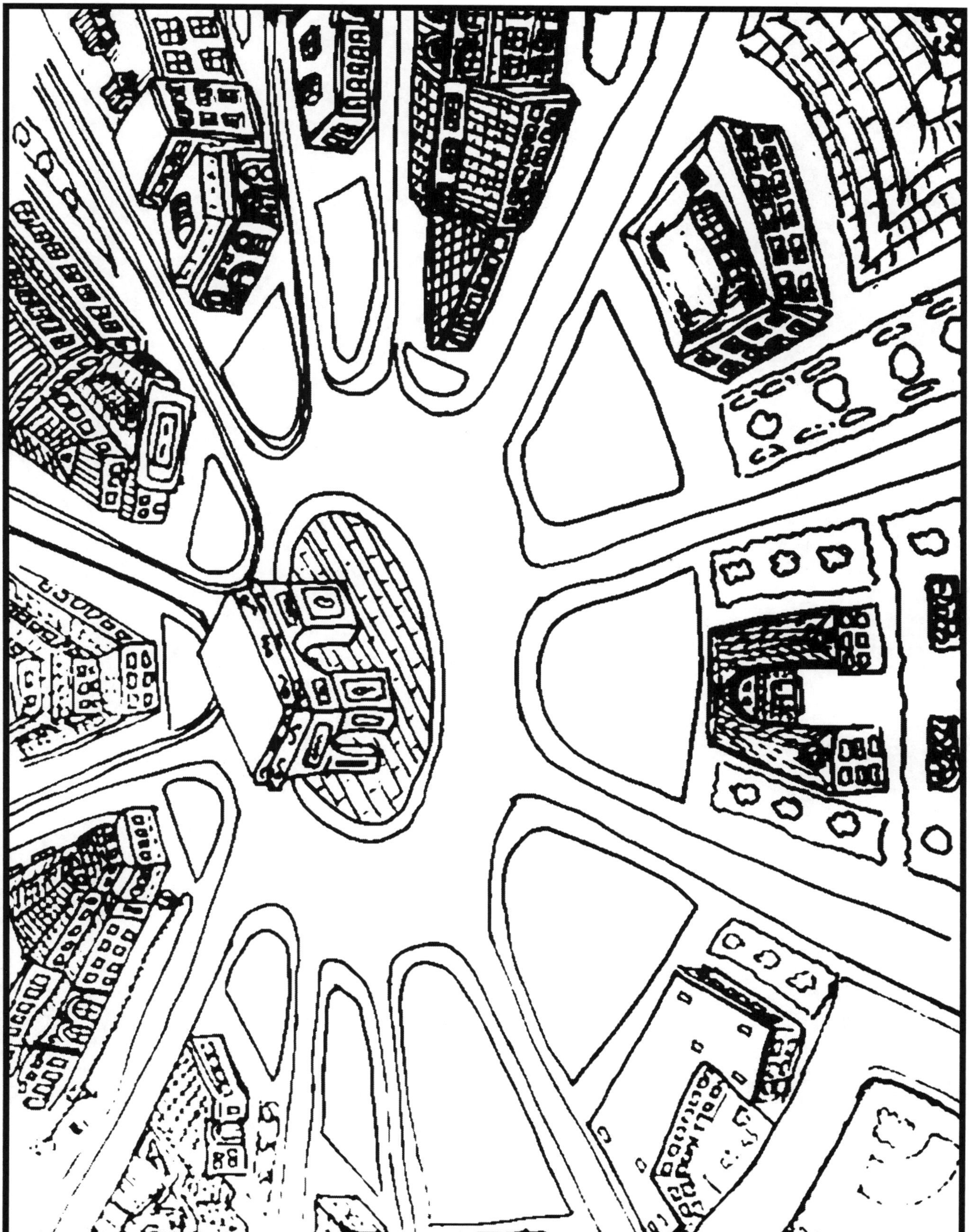

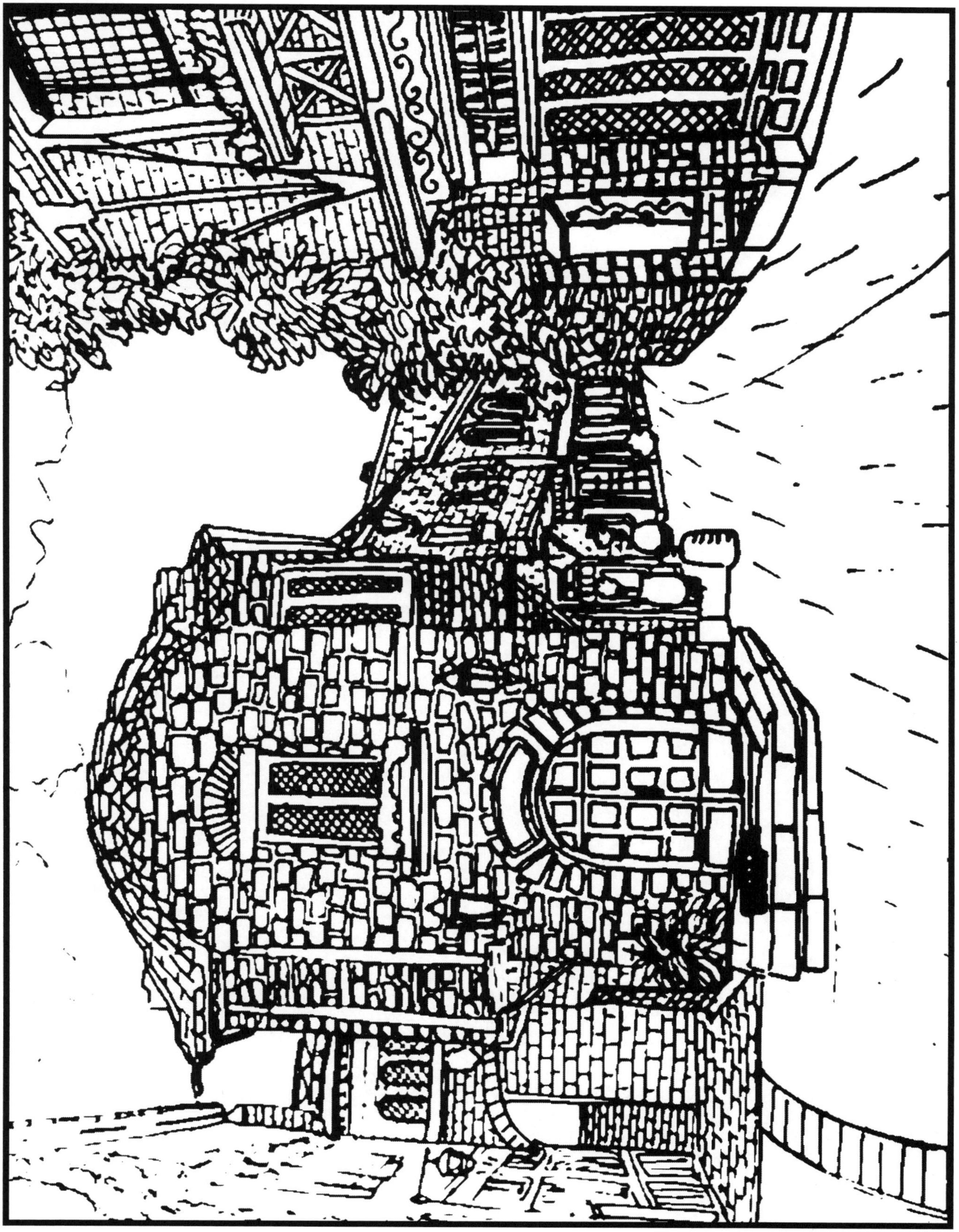

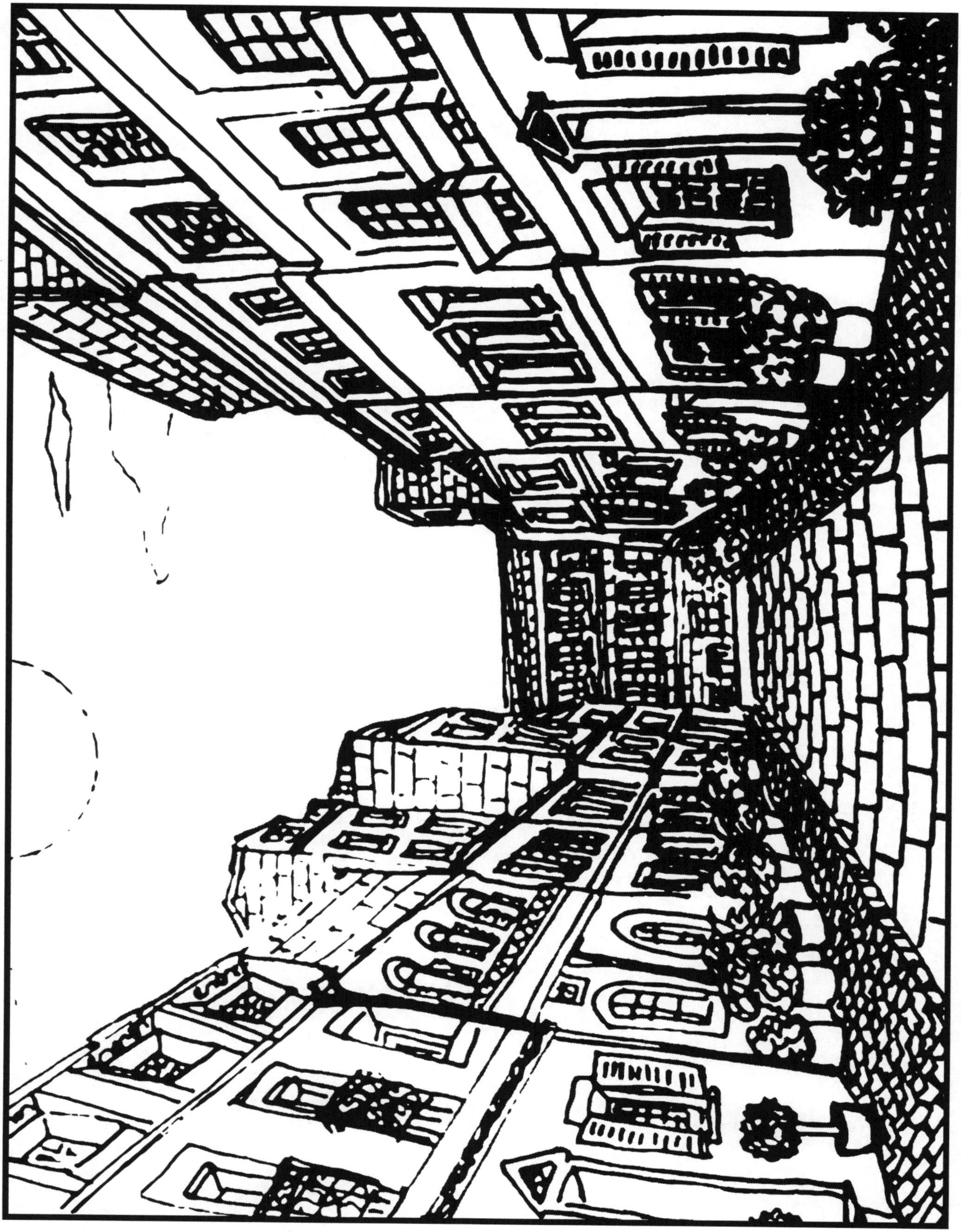

PARIS

LE CONSULAT
Paris

LADUPEE

MOULIN ROUGE
DU
LIN ROUG
1
Féerie

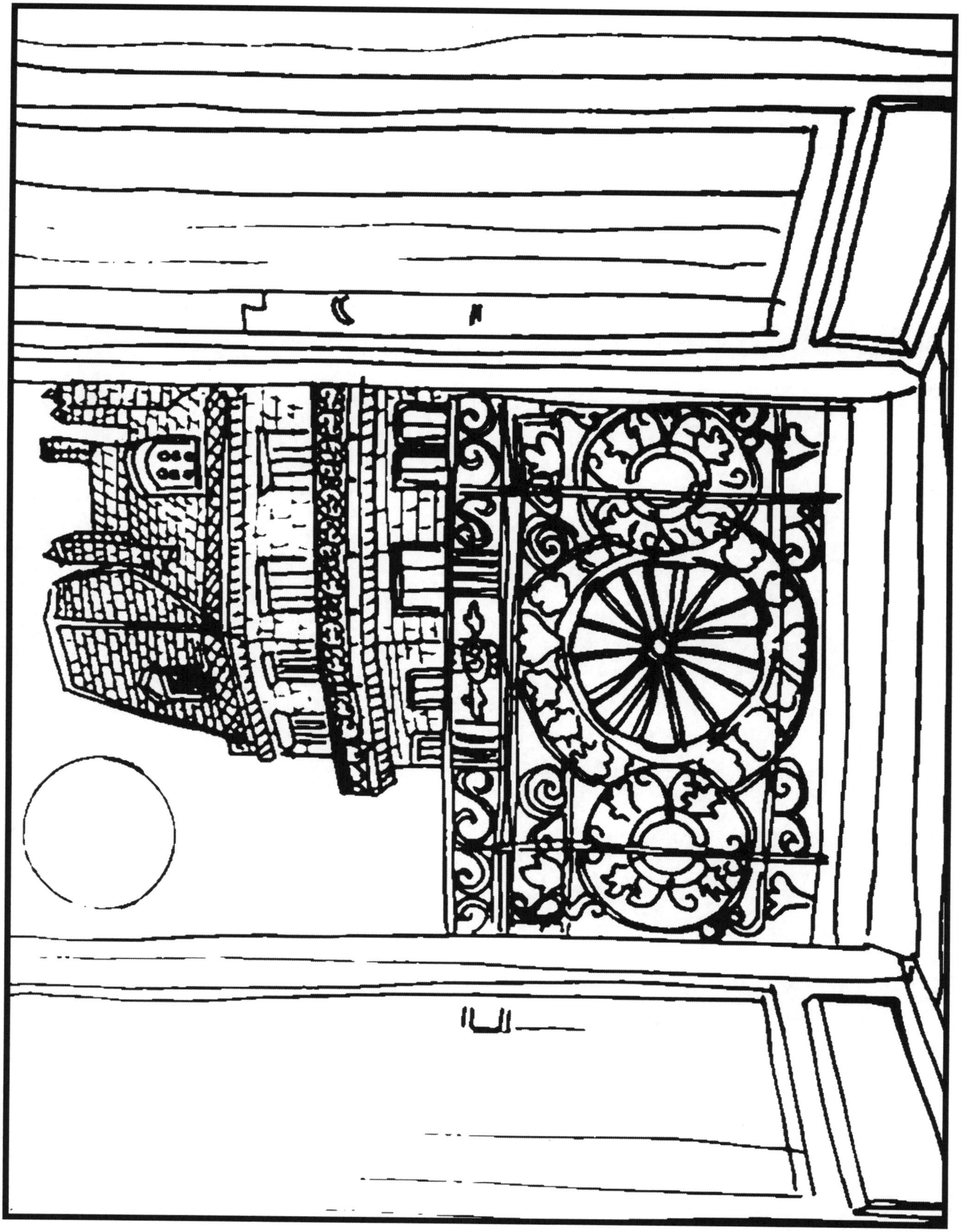

AVENUE
DE SELVES

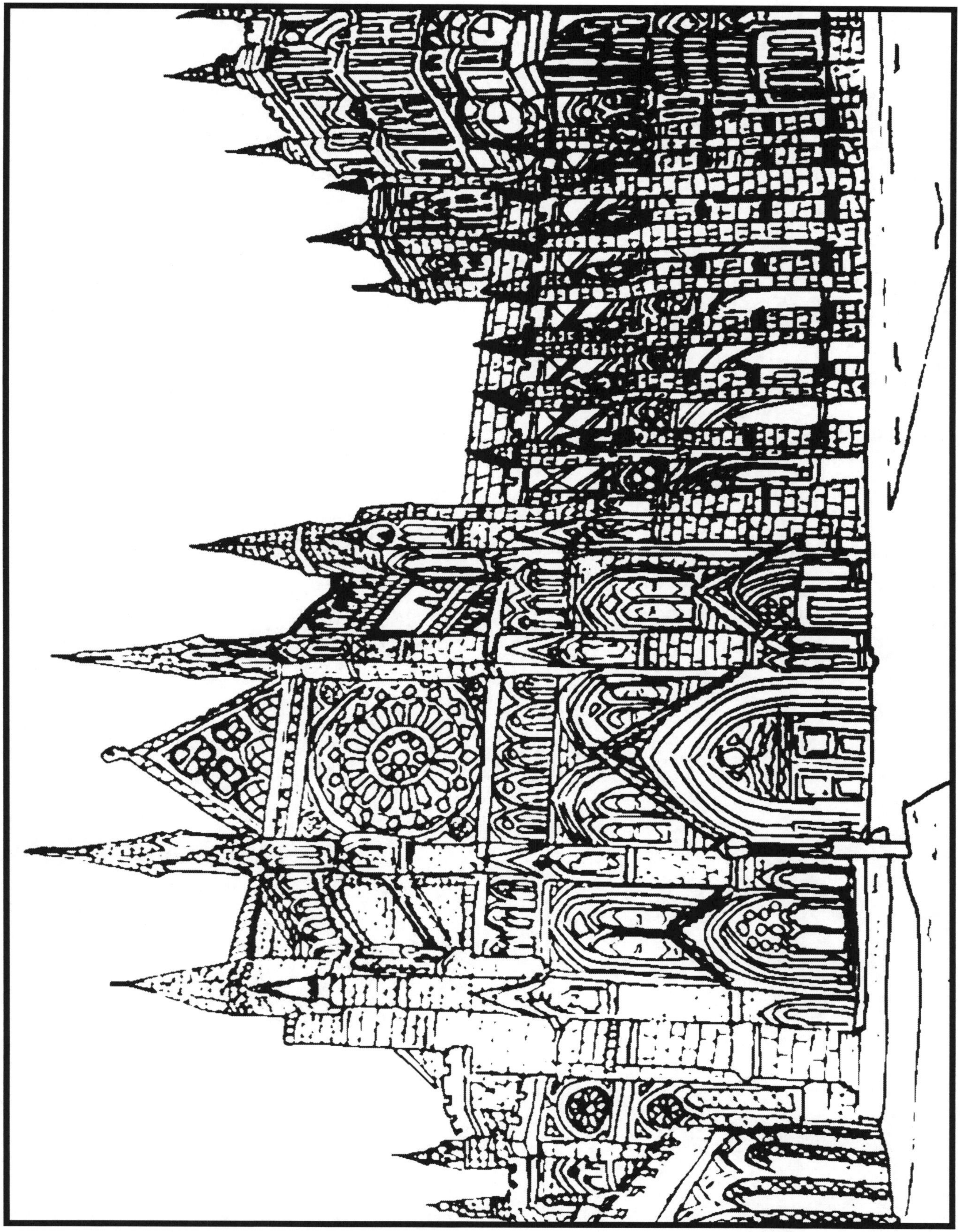

PARIS
I Love Paris
PARIS
Je t'aime

PONT
NOTRE DAME

70145608R00037

Made in the USA
Lexington, KY
09 November 2017